Organisation
of
Political Parties

London: H M S O

ISBN 0 11 701648 9

HMSO publications are available from:

HMSO Publications Centre
(Mail and telephone orders only)
PO Box 276, London, SW8 5DT
Telephone orders 071-873 9090
General enquiries 071-873 0011
(queuing system in operation for both numbers)

HMSO Bookshops
49 High Holborn, London, WC1V 6HB   071-873 0011 (counter service only)
258 Broad Street, Birmingham, B1 2HE   021-643 3740
Southey House, 33 Wine Street, Bristol, BS1 2BQ   (0272) 264306
9-21 Princess Street, Manchester, M60 8AS   061-834 7201
80 Chichester Street, Belfast, BT1 4JY   (0232) 238451
71 Lothian Road, Edinburgh, EH3 9AZ   031-228 4181

HMSO's Accredited Agents
(see Yellow Pages)
and through good booksellers

Photo Credits

Numbers refer to the pages of the illustration section (1–8): Mansell Collection, p. 1; National Portrait Gallery, p. 2; Conservative Party, pp. 3, 6 (bottom); Rex Features, pp. 4 (bottom), 5 (top), 6 (top); Labour Party, p. 5 (bottom); Scotsman Publications Limited, p. 7 (top); Plaid Cymru, p. 7 (bottom); Ulster Unionist Party, p. 8.

[Front Cover] Symbols used by some of the parties mentioned in the text

Contents

Introduction

The British system of parliamentary democracy is based on the party system, in which office is sought by organised political parties able to form and support a stable government. The party system itself rests on the assumption that there are at least two parties in the House of Commons, each of which is sufficiently united on matters of policy and principle to be able to form a government at any time. The parties are not registered or formally recognised in law, but in practice most candidates in elections, and almost all winning candidates, belong to one of the main political parties.

After a brief historical background of the origins of the major parties represented in the British Parliament and an outline of the modern party system, this booklet describes the organisation—both inside and outside Parliament—of the Conservative, Labour and Liberal Democrat parties. (The Liberal Democrats, whose formal title is the 'Social & Liberal Democrats', were formed following the merger of the Liberal Party and the Social Democratic Party in 1988.) The organisation of the two nationalist parties—the Scottish National Party and Plaid Cymru (Welsh Nationalist Party)—and that of the main political parties in Northern Ireland—Ulster Unionist, Democratic Unionist, Social Democratic and Labour, Sinn Fein and Alliance—is considered in separate chapters.

Historical Background

For over 150 years British parliamentary democracy has been based on a predominantly two-party system: with first Whigs and Tories, then Liberals and Conservatives, and most recently Labour and Conservatives alternating in power.[1]

Associations of like-minded people inevitably occur in any organised society when the principles and practices of government are open to public debate and discussion. In England they have existed in one form or another at least since medieval times. Yet for centuries, and long after the real power in the State had passed from the Crown to Parliament, such associations were loosely knit and short lived. They were usually formed to achieve some particular purpose, and afterwards came to an end, perhaps regrouping for some other cause. The origins of organised political parties in Britain[2] are comparatively recent. Before 1832—the date of the first parliamentary Reform Act—there was no clear-cut division in the House of Commons along modern party lines. The terms 'Whig' and 'Tory' had been in use for about 150 years to

[1] This is reflected in the layout of the House of Commons chamber, which is rectangular. The benches are opposite each other, and supporters of the Government sit on one side, opposition members on the other. This contrasts with many other national legislatures in which the seats are arranged in a circular fashion.

[2] The term 'Britain' is used informally in this booklet to mean the United Kingdom of Great Britain and Northern Ireland; 'Great Britain' comprises England, Wales and Scotland.

describe certain political leanings, but there was no party organisation of any sort outside Parliament. Even within Parliament no strong party discipline existed.

The reason for this lack of organisation lay, to a great extent, in the comparatively small size and exclusive nature of the electorate. In 1830 there were 656 Members of Parliament (MPs) in the House of Commons, slightly more than there are today, but they were returned by an electorate of only about 500,000 out of a total adult population of some 10 million. Many of the growing industrial areas were not represented in Parliament, while ancient country towns sometimes sent two members. The outcome of elections was decided by a small number of influential citizens, and not by the public at large. The personal influence of a candidate counted for more than the policy of a party; and, once elected, an MP did not have to follow a party line.

The growth of the modern party system was brought about by parliamentary reform and the gradual extension of voting rights to the whole adult population.[3] Corrupt election practices were gradually brought to an end, representation in Parliament became more fairly distributed throughout the country, and the social composition of the electorate changed. As a result it became difficult for candidates to offer themselves as individuals to the voters. Politicians, as the representatives of millions of voters able to take part in elections for the first

---

[3] The franchise was extended by legislation in 1832, 1867, 1884, 1918, 1928 and 1969 (when the voting age was reduced from 21 to 18). In 1985 and 1989 it was extended to include certain British citizens resident abroad. For further details see *Parliamentary Elections* (Aspects of Britain: HMSO, 1991).

time, began to form organised parties promising to carry out policies which their supporters were prepared to endorse.

Establishment of National Party Organisations

In these circumstances it became obvious that some form of political organisation outside Parliament, as well as within it, was essential if votes were to be won and support maintained. The first organised political parties on the modern pattern— the Conservative and Liberal parties—were, broadly speaking, successors to the Tories and Whigs of the eighteenth and early nineteenth centuries. The word 'Conservative' in its modern political sense first came into use after about 1830 and gradually became a normal expression to describe the successors of the Tories. The Liberal Party was formed towards the end of the 1850s with the support of former Whigs and other political groups.

Both the Liberals and the Conservatives created national headquarters in the 1860s. The Liberal Party central organisation began in 1860 when some Liberal MPs established the Liberal Registration Association, designed to encourage the registration of voters and the growth of constituency associations. Further steps to strengthen Liberal organisations came after a heavy defeat of the Party in the 1874 general election. In 1877 a large meeting in Birmingham (then the centre of Joseph Chamberlain's successful Liberal association) established the National Liberal Federation, with the aim of forming Liberal constituency associations. Under the Federation's rules, affiliated associations could send representatives to an annual meeting of the Federation's council, a forerunner of the annual party conference.

The Conservative Party founded the National Union of Conservative and Constitutional Associations in 1867, the year of the second Reform Act, which considerably enlarged the number of voters able to take part in a parliamentary election. The National Union became the national organisation of the Conservative constituency associations, designed to increase popular support for the Party outside Parliament. After the Conservative defeat in the 1868 general election, the party under the leadership of Benjamin Disraeli created the Conservative Central Office to encourage the organisation of constituency associations and to register candidates for elections.

The Emergence of the Labour Party
As the number of voters increased, a third party came into existence with the aim of representing working men in Parliament. As with the Liberal Party 50 to 60 years earlier, the Labour Party was the product both of a new body of voters created by legislation and of the growth of a new ideology.

The earlier parties began as parliamentary groups *within* Parliament and established organisations outside it in order to gain support and so achieve re-election. In contrast, the Labour Party began as a movement *outside* Parliament, seeking representation within it in order to further the aims of party policy. In 1893 an Independent Labour Party was formed in Bradford and, following a meeting in 1900 with some trade unions and socialist societies, a Labour Representation Committee was established to co-ordinate plans for Labour representation in Parliament. After the 1906 election the Committee became the Labour Party. Local committees were established at constituency level, but there was no individual membership; the Committee consisted entirely of affiliated organisations. In 1918 the Party was completely reorganised, with constituency Labour parties admitting individual members as well as affiliated organisations.

During the inter-war period (1918–39) the Labour Party took the place of the Liberal Party, which had last formed a government by itself in 1906–16, as the main rival of the Conservative Party. The first Labour Government held office for ten months in 1924, although it lacked an overall majority in the House of Commons. In 1929–31 the Party took office for a second time, again as a minority government. Since 1945 there have been seven Conservative and six Labour governments and almost all the members of the House of Commons have represented either the Conservative or the Labour Party. Despite considerable electoral strength in the country (see pp. 56–64), the Liberal Party did not at any one time, between 1945 and 1988, have more than 19 members in the House of Commons. Its successor, the Liberal Democrats (see p. 8), currently has 21 members in the House.

Other Parties

Other parties represented in Parliament include the nationalist parties in Scotland and Wales. The Scottish National Party (SNP) was formed in 1934 by supporters of self-government for Scotland and returned its first MP in a by-election in 1945. It subsequently lost support, but during the 1960s its membership increased and it secured a by-election success in 1967. In 1970 it won its first seat at a general election. Like the SNP, Plaid Cymru, the Welsh Nationalist Party (literally 'The Party of Wales'), made considerable advances in membership during the 1960s. Founded in 1925, it secured its first seat in the House of Commons at a by-election in 1966. It contested all 36 Welsh seats for the first time in the 1970 general election, but failed to return any members to the House of Commons. Both parties received their greatest support in the two general elections in 1974, when the SNP returned seven MPs in the February election and 11 in October, while Plaid Cymru returned two and then three MPs in the two contests. In 1979, however, both parties lost the ground gained earlier: the SNP was reduced from 11 members to two and Plaid Cymru from three to two.

A new political party was formally established in 1981 when a number of MPs and two former Labour ministers, not then in Parliament, broke away from their parties to form the Social Democratic Party (SDP). At the time of its launch, the parliamentary group of the SDP consisted of 14 MPs— 13 former Labour MPs and one former Conservative. The individuals concerned joined the Council for Social Democracy, set up in 1981 to 'rally all those . . . committed to the values, principles and policies of social democracy'. By 1982 the SDP was represented in the House of Commons by 29 MPs.

In the year of its formation the SDP entered into an electoral alliance with the Liberal Party. The two parties entered the 1983 and 1987 general elections with a joint programme. Their parliamentary candidates offered themselves as Alliance candidates who, if elected, would sit in the House of Commons as members of their respective parties. (The Alliance, unlike the Liberal Party in earlier elections, contested all 633 seats in England, Wales and Scotland.) In the 1987 general election the Alliance returned 22 members—17 Liberal and 5 SDP—with over 22 per cent of the total vote.

The Liberal Party and the SDP shared a common approach to major policy issues. Following discussions between members of the two parties about a formal union of the Liberal Party and the SDP, and after a ballot of members of both parties, in March 1988 members of the two parties merged to form a new party, the Social & Liberal Democrats. This party is now known as the Liberal Democrats and is represented in the House of Commons by 21 MPs, of whom 17 are former Liberals and two former Social Democrats; two more Liberal Democrat MPs were returned at by-elections in October 1990 and March 1991.

Following the formation of the Liberal Democrats, a separate Social Democratic Party continued to exist, comprising those SDP members who opposed the merger; it was represented by three MPs. In June 1990 the SDP voted to suspend the operation of its constitution, stating that it no longer had the levels of membership or popular support needed to continue as a national political party. The validity of this vote has been challenged by a number of SDP members. The three SDP MPs announced that they would remain as Social Democrats.

The Conservative and Labour parties and the Liberal Democrats have traditionally operated in England, Wales and Scotland only; they have not been organised in Northern Ireland and have not contested elections there. However, a number of Conservative constituency associations in Northern Ireland have recently been affiliated to the National Union of Conservative and Unionist Associations (see p. 23), and may contest parliamentary elections there. All the main political parties in Northern Ireland are locally based, and elected representatives from Northern Ireland constituencies at Westminster (the numbers of which increased from 12 to 17 in 1979) are drawn from five political parties. The largest is the Ulster Unionist party, with nine members.

The Party System

The Electoral System

In the British electoral system the country is divided into 650 single-member constituencies.[1] Representatives are elected to Parliament by the first-past-the-post (simple majority) method, which awards seats in the House of Commons to the candidates with the largest number of votes in each constituency. The boundaries of the constituencies are reviewed every 10 to 15 years to take account of population movements or other changes. Under this system the strongest party in the House of Commons may have an absolute majority of seats with less than an absolute majority of votes. The system is generally considered to favour two-party competition, especially between parties whose support is concentrated geographically, and to discriminate against parties with support spread across constituencies.[2]

In the 1987 general election, for example, support for the Conservative Party was greatest in the south of England, with the exception of inner London, while that for the Labour Party

---

[1] The number of constituencies will rise to 651 at the next general election with the creation of an additional constituency for Milton Keynes.

[2] An alternative system of voting, that of proportional representation, which in various forms is used in most other Western countries in electing their national legislatures, has been under discussion in political circles for a number of years. The single transferable vote system of proportional representation is used in Northern Ireland for European Parliamentary and local government elections.

was greatest in the north of England and in Scotland; support for the Alliance (see p. 7), on the other hand, was fairly evenly distributed throughout Great Britain. (A percentage distribution of the votes cast in each region for the main parties in the 1987 election appears in Table 1):

Table 1: Percentage Distribution of Votes Cast in each Region by Main Party

	Conservative	Labour	Alliance
England	46·2	29·5	23·8
North	32·3	46·4	21·0
Yorkshire and Humberside	37·4	40·6	21·7
East Midlands	48·6	30·0	21·0
East Anglia	52·1	21·7	25·7
South East	52·2	22·3	25·0
South West	50·6	15·9	33·0
West Midlands	45·5	33·3	20·8
North West	38·0	41·2	20·6
Wales	29·5	45·1	17·9
Scotland	24·0	42·4	19·2

Sources: *The British General Election of 1987*, by D Butler and D Kavanagh and *Times Guide to the House of Commons June 1987* (see Further Reading, p. 67).

Forming a Government

The party which wins most seats (though not necessarily the most votes) at a general election, or which has the support of a majority of members in the House of Commons, is usually invited by the Sovereign to form a government. The party with the next largest number of seats is officially recognised as 'Her Majesty's Opposition'; this has its own leader, who is paid a salary from public funds, and its own 'shadow cabinet'. Members of other parties, or any independent MPs who have been elected, support or oppose the government according to their party or their own view of the policy being debated at any given time. Because the official Opposition is a minority party, it seldom succeeds in introducing or amending legislation. However, its statements and policies are important, since it is considered to be a potential Government—and would become so if successful at the next general election.

On occasion, a minority government may be formed or arise. In some cases no one party succeeds in winning a majority of seats over all the other parties combined (as after the general election of February 1974). Following the defeat and resignation of the Government, it is customary in such circumstances for the Sovereign to invite the leader of the largest opposition party in the House of Commons to form a government. A minority government may also arise when, during the life of a Parliament, the governing party loses its majority through by-election defeats, as the Labour Government did in 1977. In both these circumstances, the Government has three choices: it may introduce only that legislation which commands the support of a majority in the House; it may make some form of arrangement with one or more opposition parties to enable it to stay in office; or it can ask for Parliament to be dissolved and for a general election to be held.

A minority government may stay in office so long as all other parties do not form a united parliamentary opposition to its policies and defeat it on a vote of confidence. Occasionally, a minority administration has made a formal agreement with another party to support it. This occurred in March 1977 when the Labour Government made a formal agreement with the parliamentary Liberal Party whereby Liberal MPs agreed to 'work with the Government in the pursuit of economic recovery'. The 'Lib-Lab Pact', as it was called, lasted until the autumn of 1978, when Liberal support was withdrawn.

The formation of a coalition government in Britain has taken place during this century only for the sake of overcoming national crises, such as the two world wars (1914–18 and 1939–45) or the economic depression during the 1930s. In a coalition, ministers are drawn from each of the parties con-cerned. The last coalition in Britain was dissolved in 1945 towards the end of the second world war.

The party system assumes that, in spite of the alternative programmes sponsored by the main political parties, there is common interest and agreement upon the maintenance of free institutions and parliamentary democracy.

The General Election of June 1987

The last general election was held on 11 June 1987, when the Conservative Party gained a majority of 101 seats over all other parties. The total number of electors entitled to vote in the election was some 43·2 million, and 75·3 per cent of the electorate voted. Table 2 shows the number of seats and votes obtained by each party at present represented in Parliament and their percentage share of the total vote. For the current state of the parties in the House of Commons, see p. 65.

Table 2: General Election June 1987

Party	Total votes	MPs elected	Candi-dates	% Share of total vote
Conservative[a]	13,763,066	376	633	42·3
Labour	10,029,944	229	633	30·8
Liberal–Social Democratic Alliance[b]	7,341,152	22	633	22·6
Scottish National	416,873	3	71	1·3
Plaid Cymru	123,589	3	38	0·4
Northern Ireland parties	730,152	17	77	2·2
Northern Ireland Parties:				
Ulster Unionist	276,230	9	12	37·8
Democratic Unionist	85,642	3	4	11·7
Social Democratic and Labour	154,087	3	13	21·1
Sinn Fein[c]	83,389	1	14	11·4
Ulster Popular Unionist	18,420	1	1	2·5

[a] These figures include the Speaker of the House of Commons, who stood as 'Mr Speaker seeking re-election'. He was, before his election as Speaker, a Conservative member.
[b] Seventeen Liberal members were elected out of 327 candidates and 5 SDP members out of 306 candidates.
[c] The Sinn Fein member has not taken his seat (see p. 45).

Party Organisation Outside Parliament

This chapter deals with the organisation outside Parliament and with the office of party leader of the three main political parties at Westminster—Conservative, Labour and Liberal Democrat. The next chapter covers organisation inside Parliament. The two nationalist parties—Scottish National Party and Plaid Cymru (Welsh Nationalist)—are considered on pp. 42–4 and the main parties in Northern Ireland on pp. 45–53.

Although there are important organisational differences, certain elements are common to each of the three main parties. Outside Parliament, the basic unit of organisation is the local *constituency association*. (However, local parties of the Liberal Democrats may cover one or more neighbouring constituencies —see p. 19.) These are usually linked together in *regional federations*. Also common to each party is a *national organisation* whose main function is to arrange an *annual conference*, which provides a channel of communication between the leading members of the party in Parliament and its supporters in the country. A further common feature is a *central office*, the national headquarters of the party, staffed by professional workers and providing a link between the party in Parliament and the party in the country. Finally, there is the *leader of the party*. The roles of the party organisation and the importance of the annual party conference, however, vary between parties.

Constituency Associations or Parties

Conservative Party

Conservative constituency associations are composed of individual members who live in, or are connected with, the constituency or have business interests there, and who give money each year to party funds. In many associations there are separate sections catering for the special interests of women; in most, there is a section for 'Young Conservatives' between the ages of 15 and 30. The Young Conservatives is the largest voluntary political youth movement in Britain.

The associations have complete autonomy in the day-to-day management of their affairs. They are free to elect their own officers, select and appoint their own agents, raise their own funds, and plan and carry out their own publicity programmes. They also conduct election campaigns in their constituencies in their own way, and adopt their own candidates for parliamentary and local government elections (the former from a list of names approved by the Party's standing advisory committee on candidates).

There is a fairly wide variety in the structure of associations throughout the country, but in most of them the principal officers are the president, the chairman, three vice-chairmen (those of the constituency political, women's and Young Conservatives committees) and the honorary treasurer. The governing body is normally the executive council, which is presided over by the chairman of the association and served by the agent in the capacity of secretary. The council deals with all matters affecting the association and elects representatives to the national and area organisations. It also appoints, annually, a number of committees, including a finance and general purposes committee and those dealing with such subjects as political education, trade union affairs and local government.

In constituencies where the Conservative Party is highly organised, branches of the constituency association are set up in each ward or polling district for conducting normal constituency work. A number of local branch members are usually named as representatives from the branch to the executive council of the constituency association to act as a channel of communication between the branch and the association as a whole.

The individual membership of the Party is around 1 million.

Labour Party

Labour constituency associations are known as Constituency Labour Parties. Within these parties branches may be formed, usually covering electoral wards in towns, and parishes or groups of parishes in rural areas. The Party has two classes of membership: affiliated organisations and individual members. Affiliated organisations include trade unions (the most important category); co-operative societies and branches of the Co-operative Party (the political wing of the Co-operative Movement—see p. 54); branches of socialist societies or professional organisations which are affiliated to the Labour Party nationally; and trades councils. Individual members must be aged 15 years or over and must be attached to the appropriate branch operating in the area where they live or, for those of voting age, where they are registered as parliamentary or local government electors. Members must accept and conform to the principles and policy of the Labour Party, and they must, if eligible, belong to a trade union affiliated to the Trades Union Congress (TUC) or to a union recognised by the General Council of the TUC as a trade union. Women's sections and branches of the Labour Party Young Socialists provide additional facilities for women members and for young members up to 22 years of age.

The constituency parties run their own affairs, elect their own officers, raise and administer their own funds and undertake their own publicity programmes. They select their candidates and appoint their agents subject to the approval of the national organisation, and conduct election campaigns in the constituency on behalf of the Party.

The affairs of the constituency parties are controlled by a general committee, which consists of delegates elected by the affiliated organisations, branches of individual members and women's and youth sections; all must be individual members of the Party.

An executive committee is elected annually by the general committee from among its own members to direct the work of the association under its supervision. The executive committee normally consists of the officers of the constituency party (the president or chairman, two vice-presidents, treasurer and secretary, constituency women's officer and constituency youth/student officer) and as many additional members as the general committee thinks appropriate. The executive committee may set up sub-committees to deal with the social and recreational aspects of the work of the constituency party, with the distribution of publicity material, and with the usual range of political activity. The estimated individual membership of the Party is around 325,000. There are an additional 5·3 million affiliated members who subscribe through their trade union organisations.

Liberal Democrats

The basic unit of organisation is the local party, usually covering a single parliamentary constituency, although some may cover more than one constituency in the same region, county, metropolitan district or London borough, subject to the agreement of the members. The minimum number of members is 50. The local party is a successor to the former Liberal Party and Social Democratic Party organisations in its area. Local parties are responsible for their own organisation, working arrangements and finance; they sponsor Liberal Democrat candidates in local and national elections. They are also expected to keep watch on the legislative and administrative work of the Government, especially as it affects the needs and interests of the district. They are responsible for directing the attention of local authorities, the public and the press to the importance of these subjects, and to the methods by which Liberal Democrats believe they should be handled.

There are very approximately 85,000 individual party members.

Constituency Agents

In each constituency, an agent is appointed by each party as the chief organiser of party activities in the area. Some of these agents are full-time salaried officials, who hold certificates (issued by the party headquarters) guaranteeing their knowledge of election law and allied matters. There are also many part-time or voluntary agents, particularly in the Labour and Liberal Democrat parties. The duties of the agent may include acting as secretary to the constituency association and serving as executive assistant to the local MP. Before elections, the agent is also expected to act as business manager to the prospective candidate and to ensure that election campaigns are conducted within the law. In constituencies where there is no full-time agent, part-time or voluntary election agents or organisers, particularly in the case of the Liberal Democrats, may be appointed. The salaries of most agents are met from constituency association funds, but the Labour Party head office contributes towards the cost of 28 agents in key constituencies, and also employs a number of organisers who cover more than one constituency.

Parliamentary Candidates

Prospective candidates are chosen by the constituency associations of each party according to its own established practice. Sitting MPs in all parties have to be readopted by their constituency associations at some point before contesting a general election.

Procedure in the *Conservative Party* is as follows: when a new candidate is to be chosen, the executive council of the constituency association appoints a selection committee to which the standing advisory committee on candidates at party headquarters submits a list of potential candidates who have indicated their wish to stand for that constituency. The names of local party members, some of whom may have put forward their own names for consideration, are also submitted. When any new local names have been approved by the standing committee, the selection committee chooses a number of candidates for interview, and produces a shortlist to appear before the whole executive council. A series of ballots is then taken, as a result of which one candidate may be recommended to a general meeting of the whole constituency association. Except on the rarest occasions, this candidate is formally adopted. In recent years an increasing number of constituency associations have presented a choice of two or three potential candidates, chosen by the executive council, to a general meeting, rather than just one recommended candidate.

In the *Labour Party*, when a decision has been made (in consultation with the national organisation) to contest an election and a new candidate is to be chosen, party and affiliated organisations within the constituency are invited to nominate a candidate. A nomination may also be made by the executive committee of the constituency association but individuals may not submit their own names. The general committee of the Constituency Labour Party then examines all nominations and proposes a shortlist. This list is submitted to an electoral college consisting of individual members and representatives of affiliated organisations. At this meeting, which is usually supervised by a representative from the Party's National Executive Committee (NEC) (see p. 26), a vote is taken by successive ballots, until one prospective candidate has obtained a clear majority of the total votes cast. The name of the selected candidate is then placed before a meeting of the NEC for endorsement.

The Labour Party requires parliamentary candidates, including MPs, to be reselected between elections. This provides an opportunity for replacement. Changes to reselection procedures are under consideration.

The *Liberal Democrats'* procedure involves the shortlisting of candidates by the executive committee of the local party or a shortlisting sub-committee appointed by it. All candidates must be included in the Party's list of approved candidates. Except in cases where the sitting MP or previous candidate is to be reselected, a specified minimum number of candidates must be shortlisted. Shortlists of two to four candidates must include at least one member of each sex (subject to there being a sufficient number of applicants of each sex). The exact form of voting is for local parties to determine but each member of the party is invited to participate. The former parliamentary candidate may be reselected by a vote at the executive committee of the local party followed by a ballot of members of the local party. The sitting MP may be reselected at a general meeting of the local party.

Regional Organisation

The constituency associations of the Conservative, Labour and Liberal Democrat parties are grouped into regional organisations which bring together party political opinion over a wide region and so are able to provide co-ordinated advice and information for the central organisation and party leaders.

The Conservative Party has 11 'provincial' areas in England and Wales, each having an area council on which all the constituencies in the area are represented. Scotland is split into three areas, each with an area council to which six representatives are sent by each constituency in the region.

The Labour Party has 11 regional councils, whose membership is open to the following bodies: constituency parties affiliated to the Labour Party at national level; county (regional in Scotland) Labour parties; trade unions affiliated to the Labour Party and the TUC at national level; district councils of nationally affiliated trade unions; co-operative societies or organisations; socialist societies affiliated to the Labour Party nationally; women's councils; and federations of trades councils. There are also district Labour parties which correspond to the areas of local government district councils.

The Liberal Democrats are organised as a federal party, with autonomous state parties in England, Scotland and Wales, all with their own national offices, staff and conferences. The state party in England is further subdivided into 12 regional parties. The federal party, which holds its own conferences, shares its headquarters, and some staff, with the English state party.

National Organisation

Conservative Party
The central pillar of the party organisation in England and Wales is the National Union of Conservative and Unionist[1] Associations, a federal organisation to which are affiliated some 560 constituency associations. Scotland has its own organis- ation, the Scottish Conservative and Unionist Association, but its 72 constituency associations are now also affiliated to the National Union. The main functions of the National Union are to advance the Party's cause, to give an opportunity for issues

[1] The word 'Unionist' in the title stems from the amalgamation in 1912 of the Conservative Party and the Liberal Unionists who had broken away from the rest of the Liberal Party in 1886 over a dispute concerning Home Rule for Ireland, in which they favoured continued union with that country.

to be debated, and to serve as an advisory body which keeps the leader informed of party opinion.

The governing body of the National Union is the Central Council, which meets once a year to debate motions which have been submitted from constituencies, areas, and national advisory committees. It also elects the officers of the National Union. Membership includes the leader of the Party and other principal officers and officials; the Conservative members of both Houses of Parliament and of the European Parliament; the members of the Executive Committee; and six representatives from each constituency association, together with representatives from the Scottish Association, provincial area councils, and national committees.

The Executive Committee of the National Union (which meets regularly) is composed of 200 members, including representatives of the provincial area councils (who, in turn, represent the constituencies in the areas) and the leader and other provincial officers of the Party. The Committee has authority to act on behalf of the Central Council in the intervals between the latter's meetings. Its functions include: recommending to the Central Council for election the officers of the National Union; approving the admission of constituency associations to the National Union; settling disputes between or within constituency associations; considering proposals on party or public affairs from the provincial areas or constituencies and forwarding them to the appropriate quarters. It also elects representatives of the National Union to the various national committees of the Party and submits an annual report to the party conference. The Executive Committee is advised by the following National Advisory Committees: Women, Young

Conservatives, Trade Unionists, Local Government, Education, and the Conservative Political Centre National Advisory Committee.

There are also a number of other central committees or boards, some of which report to the Executive Committee, and they occupy an important place in party organisation. They are: the Advisory Committee on Policy, which is responsible solely to the party leader; the Conservative Party Board of Finance; the Standing Advisory Committees on United Kingdom and European Candidates; the Examination Board (for agents and organisers); and the Superannuation Fund.

An annual conference, lasting four days, is held by the National Union every year and is the most important annual gathering of the Party. The conference is attended by the members of the Central Council and two additional representatives of each constituency—one of whom must be a Young Conservative—including certificated agents or organisers. At the conference the National Union receives the report of the Executive Committee, and debates and passes resolutions on party policy. It is not authorised to decide on policy and has no executive power; its resolutions are therefore not binding on the party leadership, but they have considerable influence. Annual conferences are also held by the Party in Scotland and Wales.

Labour Party

The highest authority in the Labour Party is the party conference, which controls the work of the Party outside Parliament, is responsible for its constitution and standing orders, and decides, in broad outline, party policy. The conference is normally held once a year for four and a half days and is attended by some 1,100 delegates appointed by trade unions, constituency parties and socialist and co-operative societies. Ex officio members, such as leading officials of the Party, MPs and prospective parliamentary candidates, and constituency party agents, take part.

Seven-eighths of the votes at the conference are held by the trade unions, distributed in proportion to the money that each union pays annually as an affiliation fee; the payment is made from union members' contributions to political funds.

The National Executive Committee (NEC) is the administrative authority of the Party and seeks to apply its policies between annual party conferences. It consists of 29 members, three of whom are ex officio—the leader, the deputy leader of the Party, and one youth member elected at the National Youth Conference. The treasurer and 25 members are elected every year at the annual conference, on the following basis: 12 members by the trade union delegates; 7 by the constituency party delegates; 1 by the delegates of socialist, co-operative and professional organisations; and 5 women members elected by the conference as a whole (as is the treasurer). The NEC elects its own chairman and vice-chairman every year. Its functions are to supervise the work of the Party outside Parliament at every level, and to report on its own work to the conference. It submits to conference 'such resolutions and declarations affecting the programme, principles and policy of the Party as, in its view, may be necessitated by political circumstances'.

The NEC works through a number of committees (Organisation, International, Home Policy, Communications and Campaigns, Women, Youth, Finance and General

Purposes, Campaign Strategy, and Disputes). Two of these (the International and Home Policy committees) have a number of special sub-committees and working parties appointed to deal with particular areas of policy or problems of current concern to the Party. The leader of the Party, the deputy leader, and the chairman, vice-chairman and the treasurer of the NEC are ex officio members of each committee; the remaining members are elected through the NEC itself.

The NEC also participates in a number of general committees with other representative Labour organisations. The Fabian Society[2] is affiliated to the Labour Party; it publishes pamphlets on social, economic, political and international issues, many of which aim to influence Labour Party policy.

Liberal Democrats
The Liberal Democrats determine party policy through the Federal Conference. This is attended by representatives of local parties, associated organisations representing youth and students, the Party's parliamentary team and the party officers. The Conference normally meets twice a year, in spring and autumn. It receives reports from the Party's Federal Executive, the Federal Policy Committee and the Federal Conference Committee.

The Federal Policy Committee is responsible for developing and presenting party policy, including the preparation of the general election manifesto. The Committee consists of the party leader, the President, five representatives of the Party in both Houses of Parliament, three principal local authority

---

[2] A socialist intellectual group founded in 1884 with branches in most cities.

councillors, two representatives of each of the Scottish and Welsh parties, and 13 members elected by the Federal Conference.

The Federal Executive, whose membership is elected on a similar basis to the Federal Policy Committee, is responsible for directing, co-ordinating and implementing the work of the federal party. Its responsibilities include establishing a Finance and Administration Committee, which manages the finances and directs the administration of the federal party, including its headquarters.

In England, Scotland and Wales the Liberal Democrats constitute separate state parties. Regional parties in England may also seek recognition as state parties but so far none have sought to. The state parties have separate organisations and hold their own conferences; together they form the federal party.

Central Offices
Each main party has a national headquarters, staffed by full-time professional workers who co-ordinate the party organisation and prepare various party publications, including general outlines of policy and pamphlets on particular topics.

The *Conservative* Central Office, along with its 11 area offices, is presided over by a chairman, assisted by one deputy chairman and five vice-chairmen of the party organisation and three treasurers. The chairman, who is appointed by the leader of the Party, is in charge of Central Office and has overall responsibility for maintaining the nationwide organisation of the Party. Five vice-chairmen are responsible respectively for parliamentary candidates, finance, international affairs, relations with Eastern Europe and the women's organisation. All these appointments are made by the leader of the Party. There is a separate Central Office in Scotland with its own chairman.

Central Office has three principal divisions: Party Campaigning, Communications and the Research Department. Smaller departments within these divisions cover organis-ation, community and legal affairs, speakers, finance, training, trade unions, local government, women and youth, and small businesses.

The Conservative Research Department, which is respon-sible to the party leader through the party chairman, plays an important part in developing party policies. On a day-to-day basis, the Research Department is responsible for briefing the parliamentary party (including the Cabinet when the Conserv-ative Party is in power) and servicing Conservative backbench committees. It provides factual material for party publicity and produces reference works. It has four major sections: economic, home affairs, political, and overseas and defence. The Inter-national Office and the Conservative Political Centre also form part of Central Office. The International Office provides brief-ing on aspects of foreign policy, maintains contact with parties of the right worldwide, assists liaison between the European Parliament and Westminster, and acts as the point of first contact with the Party for organisations and individuals from other countries, foreign journalists and diplomatic missions. The Conservative Political Centre provides political education facilities for party members and others interested in politics, through constituency discussion groups, seminars, weekend schools, and publications by MPs and others.

The headquarters of the *Labour Party* is composed of the General Secretary's Office and four directorates dealing with administration, organisation, policy development, and campaigns and communications. The chief official is the General Secretary, who works under the direction of the NEC, and is appointed by the annual conference on the recommendation of the NEC.

The General Secretary, as chief executive, is concerned with the entire work of the Party. The International Secretary is responsible for maintaining contacts with socialist parties in foreign countries and in the Commonwealth.[3] All the directorates are responsible to committees of the NEC; the General Secretary reports directly to the NEC itself.

The headquarters of the *Liberal Democrats* is responsible to the Finance and Administration Committee, which consists of the treasurer, the president, the vice-presidents, the Federal Chief Executive, two elected representatives of staff employed by the federal party, and five members elected by the Federal Executive. The Federal Executive appoints a salaried General Secretary, who is responsible for the employment of the staff of the federal party. Federal and English party staff currently share the same headquarters and are organised into seven departments: General Secretary's; membership and direct mail; finance; campaigns and elections; policy; conference; and party newspaper.

Party Finance
The main parties receive their funds from various sources. The central income of the Conservative Party comes from voluntary

[3] The Labour Party is a member of the Socialist International, which consists of over 90 labour, socialist and social democratic parties in various countries throughout the world.

subscriptions consisting of individual as well as company contributions. Additional contributions from the constituency associations are assessed on an agreed basis. There is no fixed subscription.

Over 70 per cent of the income of the Labour Party is provided by annual affiliation fees for each member paid by trade unions. The remainder is provided by the constituency associations on the basis of individual membership, each individual member paying a minimum annual subscription of £10, with reduced rates of £3 for students, the elderly and the unemployed, and from socialist societies and one large co-operative society.

The Liberal Democrats' funds consist of subscriptions from individual members of the local parties. The Federal Conference determines the proportion of the state parties' subscriptions which it receives. Each state party's conference similarly determines the division between its own, and the local parties' funds.

In 1990 the Conservative Party received a central income of just over £9 million; the Labour Party's central income was just under £6 million; and the central income of the Liberal Democrat headquarters in London was about £1·3 million.

No political party is legally obliged to publish its accounts. However, business firms required to publish their accounts under the Companies Act 1967 must show the amounts of contributions above £200 made to political party funds.

The Party Leaders

The power of the party leaders and the method of their appointment differ among the parties. However, in all cases, when a party wins a general election, it is the leader who is called upon by the Sovereign to form a government. As Prime Minister he or she is then entitled to choose the members of the administration.

In the Conservative Party, the party leader is elected by Conservative MPs in a secret ballot. In the Labour Party, the leader's appointment is decided on a broader basis—through election at party conference by representatives of the affiliated trade unions, the constituency parties, and the parliamentary party. The Liberal Democrats' party leader, and its president, are elected by a postal vote by party members.

Once elected, the leaders of the Conservative, Labour and Liberal Democrat parties become the national leaders of their parties inside and outside Parliament.

The leader of the Conservative Party is the Prime Minister, Mr John Major, MP (elected as leader in 1990), while the leader of the Labour Party is Mr Neil Kinnock, MP (elected in 1983). Mr Paddy Ashdown, MP, became the first elected leader of the Liberal Democrats in 1988.

Conservative Party

The leader is subject to annual re-election within 28 days of the opening of a new parliamentary session, or within six months of a general election. The Conservative leader is elected by Conservative MPs, who nominate candidates.

If necessary, there are three ballots. A candidate is elected on the first ballot if he or she receives both an overall majority of votes and 15 per cent more of the total vote than any other candidate. Conservative constituency associations, Conservative peers and Conservative members of the European Parliament are given an opportunity to make their views known. If no winner emerges on the first ballot, a second one is held and nominations for the first are void. Candidates who did not stand in the first ballot may stand in the second. The winner of the second ballot is the candidate receiving more than 50 per cent of votes. If there is no second ballot winner, a third ballot may be organised. The three candidates receiving the highest number of votes at the second ballot go forward to the final ballot, where voters indicate their first and second choices. The candidate with the lowest number of first preferences is eliminated and the votes of those giving him or her as their first preference are redistributed among the other two in accordance with their second preferences.

Once the result of the election has been declared, the winner is presented for confirmation as leader of the Conservative Party to a meeting of Conservative MPs and peers, adopted parliamentary candidates and members of the Executive Committee of the National Union of Conservative and Unionist Associations.

The Conservative Party leader is responsible for the formulation of party policy. Although kept constantly aware through the various party organisations of the feelings and opinions of Conservative supporters throughout the country, the party leader is not normally required to report on his or her work either inside or outside Parliament. The Conservative leader normally attends most sessions of the Party's annual conference and addresses the representatives.

When the Party is in opposition the Conservative leader chooses a 'shadow cabinet' of about 18 MPs and peers to serve as a consultative committee. The leader is also in charge of the party headquarters with the right to appoint all its officers. The powers of the Conservative leader are exercised only with the consent of the Party; if there is clear evidence that this consent is being withdrawn, the leader has no alternative but to resign.

Labour Party

The leader of the Labour Party, like that of the Conservative Party, is subject to annual re-election when in opposition. When the Party is in office, elections for the leadership take place only when a vacancy occurs through the death or resignation of the Prime Minister.

Candidates for election to the Labour Party leadership must be MPs and must be nominated by 20 per cent of the parliamentary party. They are elected by an electoral college consisting of representatives from the affiliated trade unions, the constituency parties and the House of Commons members of the parliamentary party in ratios of 40:30:30 respectively. The successful candidate is the one who receives an overall majority of the votes cast, and successive ballots are held until this occurs. If after the first ballot no candidate has an overall majority, the candidate with the lowest vote drops out (or the two or three lowest-placed candidates if their combined votes amount to fewer than those of the candidates above them). After the first ballot, other candidates may withdraw if they wish, but no new candidate may be nominated. The deputy leader of the Party is elected annually in the same way.

The function of the Labour Party leader is to implement, as far as possible, the programme determined jointly by the Parliamentary Labour Party and the party organisations. He or she attends the annual party conference to report on the work done in Parliament during the previous year. When leader of the Opposition, the party leader works with a 'shadow cabinet' (the Parliamentary Committee, see p. 39) whose members are chosen by the Parliamentary Labour Party. The leader appoints the official spokesmen from the members of the elected Parliamentary Committee and other members of the Parliamentary Labour Party. The leader and his or her deputy are ex officio members of the National Executive Committee, which directs the operations of the party headquarters, but he or she is not in personal control.

Liberal Democrats

Unless postponed by a vote of two-thirds of the Federal Executive, elections for the leader of the Party have to be held every two years. Otherwise an election is held either at the leader's own request or in the following circumstances: if the leader loses his or her seat in Parliament; if a majority of Liberal Democrat MPs pass a vote of no confidence in the leader; or at the request of 75 local parties following the holding of general meetings at which a quorum of members is present.

Candidates for the Liberal Democrat leadership must be members of the party in the House of Commons, proposed and seconded by Liberal Democrat MPs, and supported by 200 party members in 20 local parties or youth or student associated organisations following the holding of general meetings.

Elections for the post of president of the party are held every two years. The president chairs the Federal Executive.

Party Organisation Inside Parliament

The Whips

In Parliament the parties are managed by officers known as 'Whips',[1] who are MPs and peers (chosen within their parliamentary party). Their duties include informing members of forthcoming parliamentary business, maintaining the party's voting strength by ensuring that members attend important debates and support their party in divisions (the taking of votes), and passing on to the party leadership the opinions of backbench members.

In the House of Commons the party whips consist of the Chief Whip and, in the two main parties, the Deputy Chief Whip and a varying number of junior whips, all of whom are MPs. Those of the party in power are known as Government Whips and are paid out of public funds.

There are Government and Opposition Whips in both Houses of Parliament, but the whips in the House of Lords are less exclusively concerned with party matters and, unlike those in the Commons, may act as government spokesmen and women.

---

[1] The term 'whip' derives from fox-hunting, where whippers-in or whips are used by a hunt to look after the hounds and prevent them from straying. It also applies to the weekly circular letter sent out by each Chief Whip to all members within the same party, notifying them of parliamentary business and requesting their attendance at appropriate times.

The Government Chief Whip is directly answerable to the Prime Minister and the Leader of the House of Commons. Subject to the Cabinet, the overriding responsibility for the progress of the Government's legislative programmes rests with the Leader of the House. Under the authority of the Leader, the Government Chief Whip in the Commons attends the Cabinet and makes the day-to-day arrangements for the Government's programme of business (estimating the time likely to be required for each item and discussing the proposed business arrangements with the Opposition). The Chief Whip is also responsible for securing majorities for the Government. He or she is assisted by a very small Civil Service staff, headed by the Private Secretary, who is frequently consulted by the Leader of the House. The Opposition Chief Whip carries out similar duties for his or her own party, and also receives a special salary. Two other Opposition Whips in the House of Commons also receive official salaries.

The Government and Opposition Chief Whips meet frequently. Together they constitute the 'usual channels' often referred to in the House of Commons when the question of finding time for debating an issue or other parliamentary arrangements are discussed.

The Opposition Chief Whip receives advance notice of the Government's programme each week, and no final decision is taken until after he or she has met the Government Chief Whip. The junior whips are responsible for keeping in touch with individual MPs and passing on their opinions to the Chief Whip. There are about 12 whips on each side, each responsible for 20 to 30 MPs, usually grouped on a regional basis.

In the House of Lords both the Government Chief Whip and the Opposition Chief Whip receive a salary from public funds. The Government Chief Whip is assisted by Government Whips who, as in the House of Commons, are paid; the Opposition Whips are not paid an official salary.

Party Organisation

The most important organ of the Conservative Party in Parliament is the Conservative and Unionist Members' Committee, popularly known as the 1922 Committee. This Committee, named after the year in which it was formed, normally meets once a week and consists of the entire backbench membership of the Conservative Party in the House of Commons. It is not authorised to decide policy or to control directly the activities of the Party's leader or front bench. However, it serves to represent Conservative opinion in the House of Commons, and it is upon this Committee's support that the leader's position in the Party depends. The Committee is autonomous and independent; it has its own organisation and its own members. When the Conservative Party is in office, ministers attend its meetings by invitation and not by right; but when the Conservatives are in opposition, all members of the Party may attend meetings. The Committee is presided over by a chairman (elected annually), two vice-chairmen, two secretaries and a treasurer. Together with 12 others elected by the Committee from among its members these constitute an executive committee. This meets weekly, immediately before the meeting of the full Committee. Major issues of party or government policy are discussed at meetings of the 1922 Committee, but votes are not normally taken. Instead the chairman is expected to interpret 'the sense of the meeting'. There are no members of the House of Lords in the 1922 Committee: Conservative peers hold their meetings separately as members of the Association of Conservative Peers. When the Party is in opposition, the leader appoints the consultative committee which acts as the Party's 'shadow cabinet' and is separate from the executive committee of the 1922 Committee.

The Parliamentary Labour Party (PLP) is composed of all Labour members in both Houses of Parliament. When the Labour Party is in office, a Parliamentary Committee acts as a channel of communication between the Government and its backbenchers in both Houses. Half of the Committee is elected by the backbench Labour members of the House of Commons and the remainder are representatives of the Government. These include the Leader of the House, the Government Chief Whip and four others, including a Labour peer, appointed by the party leader. When Labour is in opposition, the PLP is organised under the direction of the elected Parliamentary Committee (the 'shadow cabinet') consisting of six ex officio members. These are the leader of the party, the deputy leader, the chair of the parliamentary party, the Labour Chief Whips from both Houses of Parliament, and the leader of the Labour peers. Its other members are 18 elected representatives of Labour MPs and one elected representative of the Labour peers. For ballot papers to be valid in this election three votes must be cast for women candidates if three or more are nominated.

Meetings of the PLP, at which broad outlines of policy are discussed and important decisions sometimes taken, are held at least twice a week, and may be convened more often. The party leader and his or her colleagues are expected to attend and do so whenever possible, whether the Party is in or out of office. In general, the PLP has a greater measure of influence over policy than its Conservative counterpart.

The Liberal Democrats meet each week to discuss forthcoming parliamentary business and other matters; the leader takes the chair. All MPs and several peers attend.

Party Committees

As well as attending party meetings, both Conservative and Labour MPs have a policy committee system, organised around subject areas roughly corresponding to those of government departments. Both main parties have about 20 groups of this kind, including, for instance, agriculture and food, economic affairs and finance, trade and industry, education, science and technology, aviation, foreign and Commonwealth affairs, and overseas development. In the Parliamentary Labour Party there are also regional groups. The Liberal Democrats' Federal Policy Committee establishes policy working groups to prepare policy papers to be debated by conference, and to provide policy advice to MPs and peers.

Financial Assistance to Opposition Parties

Annual financial assistance is given from public funds to help opposition parties carry out their parliamentary work at Westminster. The amounts provided are based on a formula related to votes received and seats won at the previous general election. The amounts payable have been revised on five occasions since the inception of the scheme in 1975. The last rise was effective from June 1987.

Assistance is limited to parties which had at least two members elected at the previous general election, or one member elected and a minimum of 150,000 votes cast. The amount given is £2,550 for every seat won and £5·10 for every 200 votes. The Liberal Democrats and the former Social Democratic Party (see p. 1) have received assistance on the basis of a formula whereby the Liberal Democrats receive the entitlement of the former Liberal Alliance and two-fifths of the former SDP Alliance's entitlement. The Social Democrat MPs receive the remaining three-fifths of the SDP Alliance's entitlement.

The amounts payable in 1988 to each opposition party were as follows: Labour Party £839,135; Liberal Democrats £139,965; Social Democratic Party £72,633; Scottish National Party £21,812; Plaid Cymru (Welsh Nationalist) £6,034; Ulster Unionist Party £39,887; Democratic Unionist Party £6,796; Social Democratic and Labour Party £2,270. Parties are accountable for expenditure to the Accounting Officer of the House of Commons. The allocation of a party's entitlement between its work in the House of Commons and the House of Lords is decided by the party itself.

The Nationalist Parties: Scottish National Party and Plaid Cymru

The Scottish National Party (SNP) and Plaid Cymru (Welsh Nationalist) each returned three members to Parliament in the 1987 general election.[1] The SNP received 416,873 votes or 14 per cent of the total vote in Scotland; Plaid Cymru received 123,589 votes or 7·3 per cent of the total vote in Wales.

The organisation of the two parties, which has many features in common, is outlined below.

Branches and Constituency Associations

The basic unit of organisation in both the Scottish National Party and Plaid Cymru is the branch, rather than the constituency association. This is partly due to the large geographical area of many constituencies in the rural regions of Scotland and Wales, which makes it convenient to organise parties at a more local level. Delegates from the branches of both parties are appointed to the constituency associations. Both the SNP and Plaid Cymru consist of individual members who pay an annual membership fee; the SNP also has three affiliated organisations. In both parties parliamentary candidates are chosen by the constituency associations in consultation with their respective National Executive Committees.

---

[1] There are at present five SNP MPs (see p. 65).

National Organisation

The annual conference of the SNP is its 'supreme governing body'. The National Council, which meets at least three times a year, is the Party's governing body between conferences. Delegates to the annual conference and National Council are appointed by their branches and constituency associations. Three affiliated organisations—the Federation of Student Nationalists, the Young Scottish Nationalists and the SNP Trade Union Group—are also represented.

The annual conference of Plaid Cymru is the supreme authority within the Party. Between conferences, which are attended by delegates from the branches, the National Council assumes responsibility for taking policy decisions. It comprises two representatives from each constituency, together with prospective parliamentary candidates and national officials. Management and finance decisions are taken by the Party's National Executive Committee, which meets monthly and comprises elected national officers and representatives of the county organisations.

Central Offices

The headquarters of the SNP comprises five departments: organisation, administration, press, research, and publications. Plaid Cymru has a national office with a general secretary and executive secretary dealing with public relations, election organisation, finance and internal administration.

Party Finance

About two-thirds of the SNP's central income is derived from membership subscriptions; the Party does not publish an annual income figure. Three-quarters of Plaid Cymru's total income comes from donations other than those from the constituency parties, and from miscellaneous sources, including the sale of literature. The Party's turnover in 1988–89 was an estimated £207,000.

Party Leaders

In the SNP the offices of leader of the Party in the country and leader of the MPs in the House of Commons may be separate. The leader of the SNP members in the House of Commons is responsible for the day-to-day tactics of the Party in Parliament, within the broad policy framework agreed by the Party's annual conference. The leader of the Party outside the Commons, however, is the National Convener, who is elected (or re-elected) annually by the party conference. He or she is responsible for the Party's overall organisation. The leader of the SNP in the House of Commons is Mrs Margaret Ewing, MP, who was elected in 1987, and the National Convener and leader of the Party is Mr Alex Salmond, MP, elected in 1990.

The leader of Plaid Cymru, known as the president, need not necessarily be an MP. Elections of the president and vice-president take place by ballot held in party branches and area meetings. The election is for a two-year term. The current president of Plaid Cymru is Dr Dafydd Elis Thomas, MP, who was first elected in 1983. He is to be succeeded by Mr Dafydd Wigley, MP, in late 1991.

THE HUMOURS OF ELECTIONEERING

1. *Each unconscious of the Other wends his Way, when some Urchin raises a Party Cheer, which soon creates Counter Cries*

2. *The Sandwich-Men are Hooted, Cheered, and Urged On. They make a Rush, Wild and Furious*

3. *With this Result*

4. *Mr. Miles Spooner Canvasses the Slums, and finds it convenient to take Two Prize Fighters with him*

5. *The Captain undertakes to Canvass the Village*

6. *Hodge Perplexed*

Mr Brown.   Conservative
Mr Smith.   Liberal
Mr Jones.   Liberal-Unionist
Mr Robinson { Conservative
             { Home-ruler
             { Radical
             { Prohibitionist
             { Nationalist
             { ...dstonite

1886

A nineteenth-century political cartoon. The two main parties at the time were the Liberals and the Conservatives (see p. 4).

J. Keir Hardie, one of the founding fathers of the Labour movement. Keir Hardie was first elected to Parliament in 1892.

A Conservative Party poster used during the Ribble Valley by-election of March 1991.

The Right Honourable Neil Kinnock, MP, the Labour Party leader, being interviewed outside the Labour Party headquarters in London (see Party Addresses, p. 66).

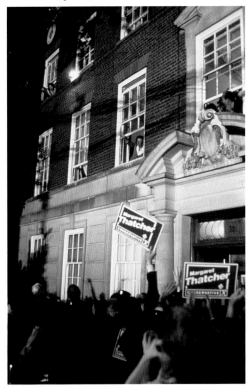

Election night, 1987, outside the Conservative Party headquarters in London (see Party Addresses, p. 66).

A Liberal Democrat Party Conference (see p. 27).

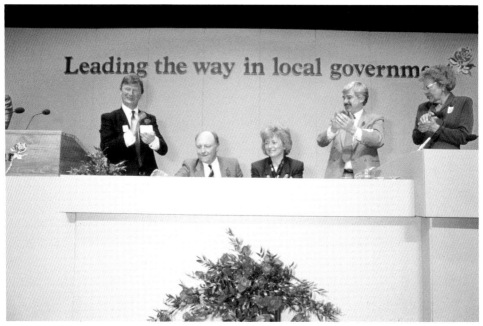

Leading the way in local governm...

A Labour Party Local Government Conference in Cardiff. In addition to the main annual party conference the major parties hold a number of other gatherings and meetings in the course of each year.

An Alliance Committee Room acting as a local campaign headquarters during the 1987 general election.

The Right Honourable Peter Brooke, MP, (left), then Conservative Party Chairman, campaigning with Conservative candidate Shelagh Roberts in the 1989 European parliamentary elections.

A Scottish National Party rally in Edinburgh.

A Plaid Cymru (Welsh Nationalist) annual conference being addressed by
Mr Dafydd Elis Thomas, MP, the Party President.

JOIN THE ULSTER UNIONIST PARTY

IT SERVES ULSTER   IT SERVES YOU
IT MAINTAINS THE UNION

FOR FURTHER INFORMATION CONTACT
UNIONIST PARTY HQ, BELFAST: (0232) 324601

OR

ONE OF OUR **NINE** MEMBERS OF PARLIAMENT
ONE OF OUR **194** DISTRICT COUNCILLORS
OUR EUROPEAN MEMBER OF PARLIAMENT
ONE OF OUR **THOUSANDS OF PARTY MEMBERS**

YOUR LOCAL CONSTITUENCY OFFICE/ADVICE CENTRE

AT ....

YOU WILL BE MADE WELCOME

PUBLISHED BY THE ULSTER UNIONIST PARTY, 3 GLENGALL STREET, BELFAST BT12 5AE.   PRINTED BY T. H. JORDAN, 14 MILLAR STREET, BELFAST BT6 8JZ

An Ulster Unionist Party poster.

Northern Ireland Parties

Members of Parliament representing Northern Ireland constituencies belong to political parties organised separately from those in the rest of Britain.

There are two major Unionist parties, representing most of the Province's Protestant community, and committed to the maintenance of Northern Ireland's union with Great Britain. The Ulster Unionist Party is the descendant of the party which provided the Government of Northern Ireland from 1921 to 1972 when the Stormont Parliament was prorogued (discontinued without being dissolved) and direct rule from Westminster introduced. The second major Unionist party, the Democratic Unionist Party, was formed in 1971.

The Social Democratic and Labour Party, the main Nationalist party, attracts support from most of Northern Ireland's Catholic community and aspires eventually towards a constitutionally achieved united Ireland. The Party was founded in 1970.

The Alliance Party, launched in 1970, attracts support from both Unionist and Nationalist communities, but has not been successful in Westminster elections.

Sinn Fein supports the campaign of the Provisional Irish Republican Army (IRA), a terrorist organisation. It has not taken up the one Westminster seat it has held since 1983.

At the general election in June 1987 the 17 Northern Ireland seats were distributed as follows: Ulster Unionist 9;

Democratic Unionist 3; Ulster Popular Unionist 1; Social Democratic and Labour 3; Sinn Fein 1. The Ulster Unionists and Democratic Unionists formed a pact before the election and did not put up rival candidates in individual constituencies. Neither party contested the seat of the Ulster Popular Unionist member, Mr James Kilfedder, the only MP at Westminster to have been elected without the support of a party machine.

The total number of votes gained by the five main political parties in Northern Ireland and their percentage of the total vote in the Province in the 1987 general election are as shown in Table 1.

Table 1: Northern Ireland Parties

Party	Total votes	Percentage of total vote
Ulster Unionist	276,230	37·8
Democratic Unionist	85,642	11·7
Social Democratic and Labour	154,087	21·1
Sinn Fein	83,389	11·4
Alliance	72,671	10·0

Branches and Constituency Associations

Outside Parliament, the basic units of organisation in the *Ulster Unionist Party* are the local branches, which are based mainly on local government electoral wards. A number of branches together form the local constituency association, which elects its own officers and delegates for the Council and Party Executive, as well as selecting candidates for parliamentary elections.

In the *Democratic Unionist Party* membership of the local branch is open to anyone aged 18 years or over who is on the electoral register for the area covered by the branch and who has given a written undertaking to support the constitution and rules of the Party. Each branch elects its own officers annually and is allowed to decide its own rules, providing these do not conflict with the party constitution and rules. Branches are affiliated to the local constituency association, which meets at least three times a year. Full members elect annually the leading officers of the association and whatever other officers they think appropriate. They also elect four members to represent the constituency on the Central Executive Committee (see p. 50–51). Each association has a standing committee with over-all responsibility for organising and co-ordinating its affairs, subject to the approval of the full association. It includes two representatives elected each year from every local branch within the constituency.

In the *Social Democratic and Labour Party* branches have two classes of membership: individual members and corporate members. Individual members must be attached to the appropriate branch operating in the constituency where they live or where they are registered as electors, and must support the principles and aims of the Party. Corporate members consist of trade unions affiliated to the Irish Congress of Trade Unions, co-operative societies, socialist societies, professional associations and cultural organisations. Branches appoint delegates to the local constituency council which promotes the policies of the Party, co-ordinates the work of the constituency branches, and runs an effective electoral organisation within the constituency. Branches and constituency councils elect their leading officers at an annual general meeting.

Membership of the local *Sinn Fein* branch is open to anyone aged 16 years and over provided they accept the Party's constitution and policy. An area council is drawn from local branches and several of these make up the regional councils (based on county or constituency boundaries) which meet regularly throughout the year to co-ordinate party activities. The final tier of organisation has several departments, each of which has a 'head' accountable to the National Executive.

The basic organising unit of the *Alliance Party* is the constituency association, whose territorial boundary corresponds to the district council, except in Belfast where, instead of a single association, there are eight associations covering each electoral district in the city. All associations may form one or more branches, based mainly on local government electoral wards. At an annual general meeting, each association elects its officers, and an executive committee, and delegates to the party council and to the annual conference.

Parliamentary Candidates
The selection of prospective parliamentary candidates for the *Ulster Unionist Party* begins with the placing of advertisements in the local press inviting applications. These are normally processed by the local executive or management committee, which may either prepare a shortlist or place all applicants before a selection conference. Candidates have an opportunity to address the selection meeting and to answer questions,

and voting continues until one candidate obtains an overall majority.

In the *Democratic Unionist Party* prospective parliamentary candidates are selected by the constituency association, with voting taking place by secret ballot. The names of the selected candidates go before the Central Executive Committee for final confirmation.

In the *Social Democratic and Labour Party* prospective parliamentary candidates are chosen by a selection convention consisting of delegates appointed by branches affiliated to the constituency council, and organised by the Executive Committee. A prospective candidate must be proposed and seconded in writing by individual party members, and the nomination forwarded to the Executive Committee. The candidate is elected by secret ballot, each delegate at the convention having one vote. The Executive Committee has the power to confirm or to refuse to confirm the choice of candidates.

In *Sinn Fein* prospective parliamentary candidates are selected by their constituency convention and the choice is ratified by the National Executive.

Any members wishing to have their names placed on the *Alliance Party*'s list of approved parliamentary candidates must apply in writing to the general secretary of the Party, after which the application is considered by the candidates' subcommittee. A selection meeting for the constituency, which is chaired by a constituency organiser (appointed by the Executive Committee), selects a candidate from the Party's approved list. Selection is by secret ballot using the alternative vote system, and the candidate with over 50 per cent of the votes is selected.

Annual Conferences, Executive Committees and Party Councils

The *Ulster Unionist Party* holds an annual conference organised by the Party's Executive Committee. Constituency associations and affiliated bodies may put forward resolutions for consideration; these then go before the Executive Committee, which may approve, amend or reject them.

The Party Executive comprises four delegates from each constituency association and delegates from affiliated groups, the Women's Unionist Council, the Young Unionists and the Orange Order.[1]

The governing body of the Party is the Ulster Unionist Council, which is responsible for the general organisation and promotion of the Party's affairs, including the annual election of party officers, among them the party leader. As with the Party Executive, the Council's officers are elected annually, and generally no one holds a particular office for more than two years.

The *Democratic Unionist Party* holds an annual conference which any party member may attend, but at which only delegates may vote. The conference is organised by the Central Executive Committee, and local branches and constituency associations may put forward resolutions which go before the Central Executive Committee for consideration.

The Central Executive Committee controls the day-to-day business of the Party and consists of elected members from each constituency association as well as the party leader and

---

[1] The Loyal Orange Institution of Ireland, known as the Orange Order, was founded in its present form in 1795 as an exclusively Protestant body which promised to defend 'civil and religious liberty'.

deputy leader. The leading officers of the Committee, who are also officers of the central delegates assembly, are elected annually by secret ballot from among its members.

The central delegates assembly, which confirms all party manifestos, consists of members elected by and from each local branch.

The supreme governing authority of the *Social Democratic and Labour Party* is the party conference, which decides the Party's policies. It is normally held once a year and is attended by delegates appointed both by branches and by corporate members. Each delegate attending the conference has one vote. The conference elects the leading party officers, including the chairman and two vice-chairmen. Elections are by secret ballot using the single transferable vote system.

The Executive Committee controls the Party's day-to-day organisation. It interprets the Party's constitution and implements conference decisions and develops policy between conferences. The Committee, which meets at least 12 times a year, consists of the party officers and 15 individual members elected at the conference.

There is also a Central Council, which provides a means of communication between the membership and the central organisation of the Party. It meets twice a year and includes branch representatives and representatives from each constituency council and each district executive.

The policy-making body in *Sinn Fein* is the annual delegate conference, which elects the party leader and the National Executive. The conference is made up of officers and members from throughout the various organisational tiers. When conference is not in session, the 16-member National Executive controls party policy. It meets at least monthly. The responsibility for carrying out routine business (the management of party funds and property) between meetings of the Executive falls to an eight-member standing committee.

The *Alliance Party* holds an annual conference, organised by a conference committee appointed by the Executive Committee. Those entitled to attend include all party officers, members of the Executive Committee, elected public representatives of the Party and delegates from each constituency association and other affiliated groups. The conference elects the party president, who may hold office for not more than two consecutive years, and up to ten vice-presidents; it also considers policy resolutions proposed by the Executive Committee or by affiliated groups.

The Executive Committee carries out the day-to-day business of the Party, subject to the direction of the Party Council. The Committee, which meets at least once a month, consists of the party officers and 15 party members elected by the Council. It presents a progress report at each meeting and an annual report to conference on the work of the Party.

The Party Council is the supreme governing body of the Party and decides party policies. It has at least four meetings a year, one of which is the annual general meeting of the Party, at which the Executive Committee is elected. The Council consists of the party officers, members of the Executive Committee and delegates from the constituency associations.

Party Leaders

Until 1972 *Ulster Unionist* MPs took the Conservative Whip in the British Parliament. However, since the Northern Ireland

Parliament was suspended in 1972, Ulster Unionists have operated in Parliament as an independent force and sit on the Opposition benches. The leader of the Party is elected at the annual general meeting of the Council. Mr James Molyneaux, MP, has been the leader of the Ulster Unionist Party since 1979.

In the *Democratic Unionist Party* the aims of the parliamentary party include providing a means of consultation and action for the Party's MPs, and co-ordinating the efforts of the Party. It elects officers annually from among its membership and fills any other posts it considers necessary. The leader of the Democratic Unionist Party is the Reverend Ian Paisley, MP, elected in 1971.

The leader of the *Social Democratic and Labour Party* has traditionally been elected by the Party's parliamentary group following a general election. Mr John Hume, MP, has been leader of the Social Democratic and Labour Party since 1980.

The leader of *Sinn Fein* is elected at the annual conference. Mr Gerry Adams is the present leader and also an MP. Since his election in 1983 he has not taken his seat in the House of Commons.

In the *Alliance Party*, the leader is elected by the Party Council, using the single transferable vote system. Dr John Alderdice has been leader of the Alliance Party since 1987.

Appendix 1
Principal Minor Parties

This appendix covers parties which gained approximately 1 per cent of the total vote in the constituencies they contested at the general election of June 1987.

Co-operative Party

The Co-operative Party was formed in 1917 and its first MP was elected in 1918, joining the Parliamentary Labour Party in the House of Commons. In 1927 the Co-operative Party reached a formal understanding with the Labour Party, and Co-operative Party branches became eligible for affiliation to constituency Labour parties. In 1946 an agreement was reached whereby sponsored Co-operative candidates were to run formally as Co-operative and Labour candidates, and in 1959 it was agreed that the number of Co-operative parliamentary candidates should be limited to 30. In the 1987 general election the Co-operative Party fielded 19 candidates, nine of whom were elected as MPs.

Green Party

The Green Party (known as the Ecology Party up to 1985) was founded in 1973 after the publication of *Blueprint for Survival*, a work published by the editors of the *Ecologist* magazine, which offered radical solutions to environmental problems.

In the 1987 general election the Green Party fielded 133 candidates, who together polled 89,753 votes, an average of over 1 per cent of the vote.

Communist Party

The Communist Party of Great Britain was founded in 1920. In its early years it sought to affiliate with the Labour Party but was turned down, and since 1924 the Labour Party has ruled that no member of the Communist Party can be an individual member of the Labour Party. Throughout its history the Communist Party of Great Britain has returned four members of Parliament: one member was elected for Motherwell, Scotland, in 1922 and another was elected for North Battersea, London, in 1924. Another Communist was elected for West Fife, Scotland, in 1935 and again in 1945, and a fourth was elected for the Mile End division of Stepney in east London in 1945.

In the 1987 general election the Communist Party fielded 19 candidates, who between them polled 6,078 votes and gained an average 0·8 per cent of the vote.

A party congress is scheduled for late 1991, at which changes to the name of the Party and its rules are likely to be considered.

Appendix 2
General Election Results 1945–87

The following tables show the results of the 13 general elections held between 1945 and 1987. Redistribution of seats took place in 1950, 1955, 1974 and 1983.

Table 1: General Election Result 1945 (5 July)

Party	Votes cast	MPs elected	Candidates	% Share of total vote
Labour	11,995,152	393	604	47·8
Conservative	9,988,306	213	624	39·8
Liberal	2,248,226	12	306	9·0
Communist	102,780	2	21	0·4
Common Wealth	110,634	1	23	0·4
Others	640,880	19	104	2·0
Total	25,085,978	640	1,682	100·0

Electorate 33,240,391 Turnout 72·7%

Table 2: General Election Result 1950 (23 February)

Party	Votes cast	MPs elected	Candi- dates	% Share of total vote
Labour	13,266,592	315	617	46·1
Conservative	12,502,567	298	620	43·5
Liberal	2,621,548	9	475	9·1
Communist	91,746	0	100	0·3
Others	290,218	3	56	1·0
Total	28,772,671	625	1,868	100·0

Electorate 33,269,770 Turnout 84·0%

Table 3: General Election Result 1951 (25 October)

Party	Votes cast	MPs elected	Candi- dates	% Share of total vote
Conservative	13,717,538	321	617	48·0
Labour	13,948,605	295	617	48·8
Liberal	730,556	6	109	2·5
Communist	21,640	0	10	0·1
Others	177,329	3	23	0·6
Total	28,595,668	625	1,376	100·0

Electorate 34,645,573 Turnout 82·5%

Table 4: General Election Result 1955 (26 May)

Party	Votes cast	MPs elected	Candi-dates	% Share of total vote
Conservative	13,286,569	344	623	49·7
Labour	12,404,970	277	670	46·4
Liberal	722,405	6	110	2·7
Communist	33,144	0	17	0·1
Others	313,410	3	39	1·1
Total	26,760,498	630	1,409	100·0

Electorate 34,858,263 Turnout 76·7%

Table 5: General Election Result 1959 (8 October)

Party	Votes cast	MPs elected	Candi-dates	% Share of total vote
Conservative	13,749,830	365	625	49·4
Labour	12,215,538	258	621	43·8
Liberal	1,638,571	6	216	5·9
Plaid Cymru	77,571	0	20	0·3
Communist	30,897	0	18	0·1
Scottish National	21,738	0	5	0·1
Others	12,464	1	31	0·4
Total	27,859,241	630	1,536	100·0

Electorate 35,397,080 Turnout 78·8%

Table 6: General Election Result 1964 (15 October)

Party	Votes cast	MPs elected	Candi-dates	% Share of total vote
Labour	12,205,814	317	628	44·1
Conservative	12,001,396	304	630	43·4
Liberal	3,092,878	9	365	11·2
Plaid Cymru	69,507	0	23	0·3
Scottish National	64,044	0	15	0·2
Communist	45,932	0	36	0·2
Others	168,422	0	60	0·6
Total	27,655,374	630	1,757	100·0

Electorate 35,892,572 Turnout 77·1%

Table 7: General Election Result 1966 (31 March)

Party	Votes cast	MPs elected	Candi-dates	% Share of total vote
Labour	13,064,951	363	621	47·9
Conservative	11,418,433	253	629	41·9
Liberal	2,327,533	12	311	8·5
Scottish National	128,474	0	20	0·2
Communist	62,112	0	57	0·2
Plaid Cymru	61,071	0	20	0·2
Others	170,569	2	31	0·6
Total	27,263,606	630	1,707	100·0

Electorate 35,964,684 Turnout 75·8%

Table 8: General Election Result 1970 (18 June)

Party	Votes cast	MPs elected	Candi- dates	% Share of total vote
Conservative	13,145,123	330	628	46·4
Labour	12,179,341	287	624	43·0
Liberal	2,117,035	6	332	7·5
Scottish National	306,802	1	65	1·1
Plaid Cymru	175,016	0	36	0·6
Communist	37,970	0	58	0·1
Others	383,511	6	94	1·4
Total	28,344,798	630	1,837	100·0

Electorate 39,342,013 Turnout 72·0%

Table 9: General Election Result 1974 (28 February)

Party	Votes cast	MPs elected	Candi- dates	% Share of total vote
Labour	11,639,243	301	623	37·1
Conservative	11,868,906	297	623	37·9
Liberal	6,063,470	14	517	19·3
Scottish National	632,032	7	70	2·0
Plaid Cymru	171,364	2	36	0·6
National Front	76,865	0	54	0·3
Communist	32,741	0	44	0·1
Northern Ireland parties	717,986	12	48	2·3
Others	131,059	2	120	0·4
Total	31,333,226	635	2,135	100·0

Electorate 39,798,899 Turnout 78·7%

Table 10: General Election Result 1974 (10 October)

Party	Votes cast	MPs elected	Candi-dates	% Share of total vote
Labour	11,457,079	319	623	39·2
Conservative	10,464,817	277	623	35·8
Liberal	5,346,754	13	619	18·3
Scottish National	839,617	11	71	2·9
Plaid Cymru	166,321	3	36	0·6
National Front	113,843	0	90	0·4
Communist	17,426	0	29	0·1
Northern Ireland parties	702,094	12	43	2·4
Others	81,227	0	118	0·3
Total	29,189,178	635	2,252	100·0

Electorate 40,072,971 Turnout 72·8%

Table 11: General Election Result 1979 (3 May)

Party	Votes cast	MPs elected	Candidates	% Share of total vote
Conservative	13,697,690	339	622	43·9
Labour	11,532,148	269	523	36·9
Liberal	4,313,811	11	577	13·8
Scottish National	504,259	2	71	1·6
Plaid Cymru	132,544	2	36	0·4
National Front	190,747	0	303	0·6
Ecology	38,116	0	53	0·1
Communist	15,938	0	38	0·1
Workers Revolutionary	13,535	0	60	0·1
Northern Ireland parties	695,889	12	64	2·2
Others	85,338	0	129	0·3
Total	31,220,010	635	2,576	100·0

Electorate 41,093,264 Turnout 76·0%

Table 12: General Election Result 1983 (9 June)

Party	Votes cast	MPs elected	Candi- dates	% Share of total vote
Conservative	13,012,602	397	633	42·4
Labour	8,457,124	209	633	27·6
Liberal-Social Democratic Alliance[a]	7,780,577	23	633	25·4
Scottish National	331,975	2	72	1·1
Plaid Cymru	125,309	2	38	0·4
Ecology	54,102	0	109	0·2
National Front	27,053	0	60	0·1
British National	14,321	0	53	0·0
Communist	11,596	0	35	0·0
Workers Revolutionary	3,800	0	21	0·0
Northern Ireland parties[b]	763,474	17	94	2·5
Others	87,962	0	198	0·3
Total	30,669,895	650	2,579	100·0

Electorate 42,197,344 Turnout 72·7%

[a] Seventeen Liberal members were elected out of 322 candidates, and six SDP members out of 311 candidates.

[b] All figures exclude the Ecology Party candidate in Antrim N., who is included in the Ecology figures.

Table 13: General Election Result 1987 (11 June)

Party	Votes cast	MPs elected	Candi- dates	% Share of total vote
1987 (11 June)				
Conservative[a]	13,763,066	376	633	42·3
Labour	10,029,944	229	633	30·8
Liberal-Social Democratic Alliance[b]	7,341,152	22	633	22·6
Scottish National	416,873	3	71	1·3
Plaid Cymru	123,589	3	38	0·4
Green	89,753	0	134	0·3
Communist	6,078	0	19	0·0
Northern Ireland parties	730,152	17	77	2·5
Others	32,463	0	87	0·1
Total	32,536,137	650	2,325	100·0

Electorate 43,181,321 Turnout 75·3%

[a] These figures include the Speaker of the House of Commons, who stood as 'Mr Speaker seeking re-election'. He was, before his election as Speaker, a Conservative member.

[b] Seventeen Liberal members were elected out of 327 candidates, and five SDP members out of 306 candidates.

Sources: All figures in the above tables are taken from Butler and Kavanagh: *The British General Election of 1987;* and Butler, D and G: *British Political Facts 1900–1985* (see Further Reading).

Table 14: Northern Ireland Parties Result 1987 (11 June)

Party	Votes cast	MPs elected	Candidates	% Share of total vote
Ulster Unionist	276,230	9	12	37·8
Social Democratic & Labour	154,087	3	13	21·1
Democratic Unionist	85,642	3	4	11·7
Sinn Fein	83,389	1	14	11·4
Ulster Popular Unionist	18,420	1	1	2·5
Others	112,384	0	33	15·4
Total	730,152	17	77	100·0

Electorate 1,089,160   Turnout 67·0%

State of the Parties in the House of Commons in September 1991

As a result of by-elections since the 1987 general election, and following the merger between the Liberal and Social Democratic Parties, the distribution of seats in the House of Commons in mid-September 1991 was: Conservative 368, Labour 227, Liberal Democrats 21, Social Democrats 3, Scottish National 5,[1] Plaid Cymru 3, Ulster Unionist 9, Democratic Unionist 3, Ulster Popular Unionist 1, Social Democratic and Labour 3, Sinn Fein 1, and vacant 2. Not included are the Speaker and his three deputies (the Chairman of Ways and Means and the first and second Deputy Chairman of Ways and Means) who do not vote except in their official capacity in the event of a tie. The Sinn Fein member has not taken his seat.

[1] One former Labour member joined the Scottish National Party in 1990.

Party Addresses

The following are the addresses of parties referred to in this booklet:

Conservative Party, 32 Smith Square, London SW1P 3HH.
Labour Party, 144–152 Walworth Road, London SE17 1JT.
Liberal Democrats, 4 Cowley Street, London SW1P 3NB.
Scottish Liberal Democrats, 4 Clifton Terrace, Edinburgh
  EH12 5DR.
Welsh Liberal Democrats, 96 St Mary's Street, Cardiff
  CF1 1DW.
Scottish National Party, 6 North Charlotte Street,
  Edinburgh EH2 4JH.
Plaid Cymru, 51 Cathedral Road, Cardiff CF1 9HD.
Ulster Unionist Party, 3 Glengall Street, Belfast BT12 5AE.
Democratic Unionist Party, 296 Albertbridge Road, Belfast
  BT5 4GX.
Social Democratic and Labour Party, 24 Mount Charles,
  Botanic Avenue, Belfast BT7 1NZ
Sinn Fein, 44 Parnell Square, Dublin 1.
Alliance Party, 88 University Street, Belfast BT7 1HE.
Co-operative Party, 342 Hoe Street, Walthamstow, London
  E17 9PY.
Communist Party, 6 Cynthia Street, London N1 9JF.
Green Party, 10 Station Parade, Balham High Road,
  London SW12 9AZ.

Further Reading

			£
BLAKE, Robert [Lord].			
The Conservative Party from Peel to Thatcher			Out of
ISBN 0 413 58140 3.	Methuen	1985	print
BOGDANOR, VERNON.			
Multi-Party Politics and the Constitution	Cambridge		
ISBN 0 521 27526 1.	University Press	1983	3·00
BUTLER, DAVID.			
Governing Without a Majority.			
ISBN 0 333 43489 7.	Macmillan	1986	10·99
BUTLER, D and G.			
British Political Facts:1900–1985.			
ISBN 0 333 39948 X.	Macmillan	1986	20·99
BUTLER, D and KAVANAGH, D.			
The British General Election of 1987.			
ISBN 0 333 39633 2.	Macmillan	1988	12·50
COOK, CHRISTOPHER.			
A Short History of the Liberal Party 1900–1987.			
ISBN 0 333 44884 7.	Macmillan	1989	10·99
DRUCKER, H.			
Doctrine and Ethos in the Labour Party.			Out of
ISBN 0 04 329027 2.	Allen and Unwin	1979	print
INGLE, STEPHEN.			
The British Party System.			
ISBN 0 631 172114.	Basil Blackwell	1987	9·95
KAVANAGH, D. *(ed.).*			Out of
The Politics of the Labour Party.	Allen and Unwin	1982	print

Parliament.
ISBN 0 11 701631 4.   HMSO   1991
Parliamentary Elections.
ISBN 0 11 701647 0.   HMSO   1991

Forthcoming Publications
Forthcoming titles in the Aspects of Britain series
will cover Britain's system of government, the
Civil Service and executive agencies.

Written by Reference Services,
Central Office of Information

Printed in the UK for HMSO.
Dd 295007 c40 11/91